Anton Chekhov

Little Comedies

Translation by Richard Nelson, Richard Pevear, and Larissa Volokhonsky

Adapted by Richard Nelson

Salamander Street

PLAYS

OTHER BOOKS BY RICHARD NELSON AVAILABLE FROM WORDVILLE

A DIARY OF WAR & THEATRE

Making Theatre in Kyiv, Spring 2024

ISBN: 9781399991964

In the midst of war, spending nine weeks directing his play, *Conversations in Tusculum*, in Kyiv, Ukraine, American playwright and director Richard Nelson kept a diary. Here the mundane, the artistic, and the ongoing war entwine in a visceral account of making theatre in a different world at a time and a place where it has come to have a very special meaning. A profoundly moving, exceptional, essential story, full of humor, self-questioning, confusions, doubts, fears, heartbreak, and joy, set in the middle of a beautiful, magical city under attack.

SIX YOUNG WOMEN PUTTING ON A PLAY

A Diary of Theatre and War: Kyiv, Winter 2025

ISBN: 9781068233401

With the world's politics in a mess, with an American President leading that charge, American playwright, Richard Nelson, wrote and directed a play for Theater on Podil in Kyiv, Ukraine. Throughout the ten weeks of rehearsals for *When the Hurlyburly's Done*, he was inspired by his six young actresses, some as young as twenty-one, and so they had lived half their lives in wartime. They laughed and cried as the play, their characters, their lives and the war entwined. An inspiring and very human story about making art when everything else feels out of one's control.

First published in 2026 by Salamander Street Ltd., a Wordville imprint. (info@salamanderstreetcom).

ISBN: 9781068233494

10 9 8 7 6 5 4 3 2 1

Further copies of this publication can be purchased from www.salamanderstreet.com

CONTENTS

Preface by Richard Pevear vii

Director's Note by Richard Nelson xi

LITTLE COMEDIES

The Bear 1

A Proposal 17

The Wedding 33

On the Harmfulness of Tobacco 49

Swan Song 55

PREFACE

In a famous disagreement over his last play, T*he Cherry Orchard*, in 1903, Chekhov, who was displeased with Konstantin Stanislavsky's production of it, insisted in a letter to the director's wife, the actress Maria Lilina, that the play was "not a drama, but a comedy, in places even a farce." Stanislavsky himself wrote back that it was "not a comedy or a farce, as you wrote, it is a tragedy..." I can very well imagine, however, that if Stanislavsky had staged it as a comedy, Chekhov might have insisted that it was in places even a tragedy. As the reader of this collection of his one-act plays will discover, such generic ambiguity was characteristic of Chekhov's theater works from the beginning.

Of the five one-act plays collected here, Chekhov subtitled two as "jokes." The other three are labeled one "a dramatic sketch," one "a dramatic monologue," and one simply "a play." He referred to them at times as farces or vaudevilles, and often spoke dismissively of them, but as a playwright he took the joking seriously. They were written for the most part between 1886 and 1891—that is, before the 1896 premier of *The Seagull*, the first of his four "canonical" plays: *Swan Song* in 1887-88, *The Bear* in 1888, *The Proposal* in 1888-89 and *The Wedding* in 1889-90. The one exception is *The Harmfulness of Tobacco*. His work on this monologue stretched across 17 years, from the first version of 1886, through at least five revisions, to the final version of 1903 *(the one included here)*, which he called "a completely new play with the same title..." It was not something he simply tossed off and forgot, as he sometimes liked to pretend.

Owing to its multi-cultural population, there was a rather lively theater in the provincial town of Taganrog, on the Sea of Azov, where Chekhov was born in 1860. His first visit to the theater, at the age of 13, was to see a production of Jacques Offenbach's operetta *La belle Hélène*, and the event stayed with him. Three years later he was already trying his hand at playwriting. By 1878 he had written some one-act farces and a full-length play entitled *Fatherless*, none of which have survived, though the full-length play may have become the sprawling and unfinished *Platonov (1880-81)*. He also began to turn out an enormous number of short prose sketches, which he published in various weekly humor magazines. This work helped him to support his family—elderly parents, four brothers and a sister—who by then had all moved to Moscow, where he joined them and entered medical school in 1879, graduating in 1884.

During those years, Chekhov published three collections of stories, the third of which, *In the Twilight*, was praised by important critics and was awarded the prestigious Pushkin Prize in 1888. Even before that, however, his work had been noticed by Fyodor Korsh, founder in 1882 of the first private (and fully electrified) commercial theater in Moscow. Korsh's aim was to attract a younger audience, to produce both light entertainments and works from the more serious dramatic repertoire of Russia and Europe. In 1887 he commissioned a full-length play from Chekhov, who was glad to accept. Judging by the books of stories, Korsh no doubt expected a light comedy; what he received was something else, entitled *Ivanov*. Chekhov wrote the play in less than two weeks and was pleased with it, as was Korsh, but he was not pleased with the incoherent production, nor was most of the audience, and the show was quickly taken down. That was in November 1887. On February 19, 1888, however, Korsh premiered Chekhov's oneact "dramatic sketch" *Swan Song*, and in October of the same year came his production of *The Bear*. Both were highly successful, *The Bear* especially; by March of the next year it had been staged in some 16 towns all over Russia (Chekhov liked to call *The Bear* his "milk cow"). *The Proposal* had its opening on April 12, 1889 and was also a great success; on August 9, 1889 it was performed at the summer residence of the emperor Alexander III in Tsarskoe Selo. In 1890 Korsh premiered *The Wedding.*

The aesthetics of Chekhov's plays are already present in his earliest one-act sketch, *Swan Song.* Also present is the memory of his first theater experience 15 years earlier in the playhouse of Taganrog: the central character of the sketch, the actor Vassily Vassilyich Svetlovidov, has just played Calchas, a character from *La belle Hélène*, and is still wearing his costume when he wakes up drunk in the now dark theater. Vladimir Nemirovich-Danchenko, co-founder with Stanislavsky of the Moscow Art Theater, noted of Chekhov's one-acts: "The beauty of these 'jokes' lay not only in their hilarious situations but in the fact that their characters were real people, rather than vaudeville types..." The plays are based not on comical situations and stereotyped characters, but on the reactions of ordinary people to the comical situations they find themselves in. For the first time in his life, the old actor Svetlovidov looks out into the darkness of an empty theater. He describes it as "a black, bottomless pit, like a grave with death itself hiding in it..." In *The Harmfulness of Tobacco* there is also a theater, this time not empty but filled with an audience that has come to hear Nyukhin's lecture, which he never gets around to giving, on the harmfulness of tobacco. In both cases, the play also addresses the actual audience directly: we are there in the dark theater when Svetlovidov looks out at us; we are there hearing Nyukhin avoid giving his lecture. As Chekhov's contemporary, the Russian novelist and playwright Leonid Andreev, observed about one of his plays: "We have ceased to be onlookers, ceased to be ourselves with our programs and binoculars, but have turned into characters in the play."

Chekhov's one-acts have since been performed, translated, adapted all over the world. In Japan, as early as 1909, *The Proposal* became the second production of the new Free Theater, where modern Japanese theater began. Russian stagings and adaptations also went on constantly, perhaps the most famous being *33 Swoons*, Vsevolod Meyerhold's combining of *The Bear, The Proposal*, and *The Jubilee*, produced in 1935 at his theater in Moscow. To this day these brief plays continue to be grounds for exploring the essence of Chekhov's fascinating and elusive dramatic art.

Richard Pevear
2026

DIRECTOR'S NOTE

A Note on Little Comedies

I am pretty sure that Anton Chekhov never imagined an entire evening of five of his short plays, some which he subtitled 'a joke' or 'a vaudeville.' He did not write them to make up an evening. They were written into the context of the late 19th-century Russian vaudeville—where someone sings a song, an actor recites a speech from a play, and there is a Chekhov short play mixed in. We do not have that context today. American vaudeville and the TV equivalents like the old Ed Sullivan Show are gone. I suppose the closest relative is what is called 'sketch comedy', done in Comedy Clubs. These are often improvised, and a good bit of the fun is watching how quickly the actors can think (and make up funny stuff) on their feet, live, in front of an audience. But these short plays aren't like that either; they are written plays; and if seen in this context, there is the risk of an audience finding them to be poor, drawn out, sketch comedy bits.

I know of two efforts (I am sure there have been others) to put together Chekhov's short plays into one evening. Both failed. The famous Russian director, Meyerhold, made one attempt; and he seems to have pushed the physical comedy to the breaking point. The English playwright and translator, Michael Frayn, created an evening he called *The Sneeze*; it starred a wonderful comedian (the 'Mr. Bean' in the TV show). It too proved not very funny.

So what we are attempting is, indeed, an experiment; to group these plays together, and, hopefully, end up with not just a series of skits, but rather some sort of whole. Our tack has, to my knowledge, never been tried before with these plays;

and that tack is to treat the plays as we would the full-length major plays of Chekhov (*The Cherry Orchard, The Seagull, Uncle Vanya*, etc.) That is, as plays about human beings, who struggle, find themselves in difficult straights, are lost, unaware, scared—and always recognizably human, and so like us. The 'comedy' of these 'comedies' then (and they are funny), is that of being profoundly human. And as each is quite short, hopefully they will come across not as individual 'bits' but as 'snapshots' of lives; and so when set side by side, they will portray a world. That's our hope and our experiment.

R. Nelson

The director's note for the Alley Theater production of *Little Comedies*.

CHARACTERS

The Bear

Eléna Ivánovna Popóva, a cute widow, landowner
Grigóry Stepánovich Smirnóv a landowner
Luka, a servant

A Proposal

Stepán Stepánovich Chubukov, a landowner
Natálya Stepánovna, his daughter
Iván Vassílyevich Lómov, a neighboring landowner

The Wedding

Zhigálov, minor civil servant, father of the bride
Nastásya Timoféevna, his wife, mother of the bride
Dáshenka, their daughter, the bride
Aplómbov, the fiancé
Revunóv, a retired second-class captain in the navy
Niúnin, insurance agent, and friend of the family
Zmeyúkina, midwife, and would-be singer
Zed, telegrapher, and former boyfriend of the bride
Dymba, Greek confectioner

On the Harmfulness of Tobacco

Iván Ivánovich Nyúkhin, husband of the head of a girls' school

Swan Song

Vassíly Vassílyich Svetlovídov, an old actor
Feklusha, a stage manager

Little Comedies was first produced at The Alley Theatre (Rob Melrose, Artistic Director; Dean R. Gladden, Managing Director) in Houston, Texas, on October 6, 2023. The cast and creative contributors were:

The Bear

Elena	**Melissa Molano**
Girgory	**Christopher Salazar**
Luka	**Todd Waite**

The Proposal

Stepan	**Chris Hutchison**
Natalya	**Elizabeth Bunch**
Ivan	**David Rainey**

The Wedding

Zhiglalov	**David Rainey**
Nastasya	**Elizabeth Bunch**
Dashenka	**Melissa Molano**
Aplomobov	**Dylan Godwin**
Revunov	**Todd Waite**
Niunin	**Christopher Salazar**
Zmeyukina	**Melissa Pritchett**
Zed	**Chris Hutchison**
Dymba	**Shawn Hamilton**

The Harmfulness of Tobacco

Ivan	**David Rainey**

Swan Song

Vassily	**Todd Waite**
Feklusha	**Melissa Pritchett**

Director	**Richard Nelson**
Scenery	**Michael Locher**
Costumes	**Susan Hilferty & Camilla Dely**
Lighting	**Jennifer Tipton**
Sound	**Scott Lehrer**
Stage Manager	**Kristen Larson**
Asst. Stage Manager	**Kaylee Sarton McCray**

This translation of *Little Comedies* was commissioned by the Alley Theatre.

CHARACTERS

ELÉNA IVÁNOVNA POPÓVA
a cute widow with dimples, a landowner

GRIGÓRY STEPÁNOVICH SMIRNÓV
a landowner, middle-aged

LUKA
a servant

THE BEAR

ELENA's estate. The drawing room.

ELENA in mourning, looking at a photograph, and LUKA.

LUKA: It's not good. You're destroying yourself. The maid and the cook go to pick berries, everything that has breath rejoices, even the cat knows her own pleasure, she roams around the yard chasing birds, and you stay shut up in your room all day long, like in a convent, and have no pleasure at all. It's already a year now that you haven't gone out.

ELENA: And I never will. What for? My life is over. He lies in the grave, and I've buried myself within these four walls. We're both dead.

LUKA: There we go. Really, I don't like hearing that. Nikolái Mikháilovich died, that's how it is, it's God's will, may he rest in peace. You've grieved enough, it's time to stop. You can't weep and wear mourning all your life. My old mother also died when her time came. I grieved and wept for a month, and that was enough for her. I couldn't go around weeping and wailing all my life, the old woman wasn't worth it. You've forgotten all your neighbors. You don't visit, and you don't receive. Forgive me, but we live like spiders—never see the light of day. As if there weren't any decent people, but no, the whole district's full of gentlemen. There's a regiment stationed in Ryblovo, the officers are perfect pictures, you can't take your eyes off them. And in their camp there's a ball every Friday, and nearly every day the military band plays. Young, beautiful, the very picture of health—just go and live. Beauty's not given forever. In ten years or so you'll want to strut before the gentlemen officers and blow smoke in their eyes, but it will be too late.

ELENA: You think I'm alive, but it only seems so. I swore to myself that to the very grave I would not stop mourning. Do you hear? Let his shade see how I love him. I know, it's no secret from us that he was often unfair to me, cruel, and... and even unfaithful, but I will be faithful till my grave and prove to him how I can love. There, beyond the grave, he will see me the same as I was before his death.

LUKA: Instead of such talk, it would better to stroll in the garden, or order Toby or Giant hitched up and go to visit the neighbor.

ELENA: Oh God...

LUKA: What's wrong?

ELENA: *(the photo)* Toby and him. He loved Toby so much. He always took him to go to the Korchágins and the Vlásovs. He was such a wonderful driver. There was such grace in his figure when he pulled hard on the reins. Remember? Toby, Toby. Let him have some extra oats today.

Doorbell..

(Startled) Who's that?

LUKA: I don't know.

ELENA: I don't receive anybody.

LUKA: I don't know.

LUKA Exits.

ELENA: *(Looking at the photograph)* You'll see, Nicolas, how I can love and forgive. My love will be extinguished together with me, when my poor heart stops beating. And aren't you ashamed? I'm a good girl, a faithful wife, I've locked myself in and will be faithful to you till the grave, and you... Aren't you ashamed, chubsy? You cheated on me, made scenes, left me alone for weeks on end.

LUKA: *(Enters)* Someone's asking for you. He wants to see you.

ELENA: Didn't you tell him that since the day of my husband's death I don't receive anyone?

LUKA: I did, but he refuses to listen, he says it's a very urgent matter.

ELENA: I don't receive an-y-one.

LUKA: He's some sort of demon. He curses and shoves his way past. He's already in the dining room.

ELENA: All right, ask him in. And don't forget to give Toby extra oats today.

LUKA exits.

Such boors. What a burden these people are. What do they need from me?

GRIGORY: *(off)* Idiot, you talk too much! Shut up!

ELENA: Why do they disturb my peace? It looks like I'll really have to go into a convent.

GRIGORY: (*Entering*) Madam, I have the honor of introducing myself: retired artillery lieutenant, landowner, Smirnov. I'm forced to disturb you on some very important business.

ELENA: What can I do for you?

GRIGORY: Your late husband, with whom I had the honor of being acquainted, gave me two promissory notes by which he was left in debt to me for twelve hundred rubles. Tomorrow I am supposed to pay interest to the land bank, and I would like to ask you, madam, to pay the money back to me today.

ELENA: Twelve hundred. And what was my husband in debt to you for?

GRIGORY: He bought oats from me.

ELENA: If my husband was left in debt to you, then of course I'll pay; but kindly excuse me, today I don't have any money here. My steward will come back from town in two days, and I'll tell him to pay you what's owed, but meanwhile I cannot fulfill your wish. Besides, today it is exactly seven months since my husband's death, and I am absolutely in no mood to concern myself with money matters.

GRIGORY: And I'm in such a mood that if I don't pay the interest tomorrow, I'll go down the drain headfirst. My estate will be seized.

ELENA: You'll get your money in two days.

GRIGORY: I need the money today, not in two days.

ELENA: Forgive me, I cannot pay you today.

GRIGORY: And I can't wait two days.

ELENA: What can I do if I don't have it right now?

GRIGORY: So you can't pay?

ELENA: I believe I said clearly: my steward will come back from town, and you'll get your money.

GRIGORY: I came to you, not to your steward. What the hell—excuse the expression—do I need your steward for?

ELENA: Forgive me, sir, I'm not used to these strange expressions and to such a tone. I'll no longer listen to you. *(Exits quickly)*

GRIGORY: And I'm supposed to keep calm. I met an exciseman on the way here and he asked me, "Grigory, why are you always angry?" For pity's sake, how can I not be angry? I need money.

I started out yesterday at daybreak, went around to all my debtors, not one of them paid his debt. I'm dog-tired, devil knows how I spent the night—in some falling apart eatery, by a vodka barrel. I finally make it here, fifty miles from home, hoping to collect, and what I get is her 'mood'!

A mood. Husband died seven months ago. And have I got to pay the interest or not? I ask you—have I got to pay the interest or not? So your husband died, you've got your mood and all this blech... the steward's gone off somewhere, to hell with him, and what am I supposed to do? Fly away from my creditors on a hot-air balloon? Bash my brains out against a wall? I come to Grúzdev's—he's not home; Yaroshévich hides; I have a vicious fight with Kurítsyn and nearly chuck him out the window; Mazútov has stomach problems, and this lady has her mood. Not one of the scoundrels will pay. It's because I've been too easy on them, because I'm a weakling, a wet rag, an old woman. I've been too soft. Well, just wait.

(shouts) Hey you!

(continues) You'll learn about me. I won't allow anybody to muck with me, God damn it. I'll stick around here till she pays. I'm so angry today. I'm shaking all over, I'm out of breath.

LUKA: *(Enters)* What do you want?

GRIGORY: Bring me some water! Or kvass!

LUKA exits.

A man desperately needs money, he's ready to hang himself, and she won't pay because, you see, she's not inclined to occupy herself with money matters. Real, female, petticoat logic. That's why I never liked and still don't like talking to women. It's easier for me to sit on a powder keg than talk to a woman. I've got chills in my spine—that's how furious that fancy dress has made me. The moment I see a poetic creature standing there, even from a distance, rage gives me cramps in the legs. I'm about ready to shout for help.

LUKA: *(Enters with water)* The lady is ill and is not receiving.

GRIGORY: Get out!

LUKA: She's ill and not receiving.

LUKA exits.

GRIGORY: Ill and not receiving. I'll stay and go on sitting here until you give me my money. If you're ill for a week, I'll sit here for a week. If you're ill for a year, then for a year. I'll get my own back, dear girl. I'm not going to be touched by your mourning and your dimples. We know all about dimples.

(Shouts off) Hey you!

(continues) The heat's unbearable, nobody pays, a bad night's sleep, plus this mourning dress with her mood. Headache.

LUKA: *(Enters)* What do you want?

GRIGORY: Unhitch my horses! I'm not leaving! I'm staying here! Tell them at the stable to give the horses oats!

LUKA: Staying...

LUKA exits.

GRIGORY: *(looks himself over)* A pretty sight. Covered with dust, filthy boots, unwashed, uncombed, bits of straw. For all I know, the little lady took me for a robber. I'm not a guest, I'm a creditor, and there's no dress code for creditors. I'm so angry. I think I could grind the whole world to dust.

(Shouts) Hey, you!

ELENA: *(Enters)* My dear sir, in my seclusion I long ago became unaccustomed to the human voice and cannot bear shouting. I ask you earnestly not to disturb my peace.

GRIGORY: Pay me the money and I'll leave.

ELENA: I told you in plain Russian that I don't have any money here. Wait till the day after tomorrow.

GRIGORY: I, too, had the honor of telling you in plain Russian that I need the money, not the day after tomorrow, but today. If you don't pay me today, tomorrow I'll have to hang myself.

ELENA: But what can I do if I don't have any money?

GRIGORY: So you're not going to pay me?

ELENA: I can't...

GRIGORY: In that case I'll stay and go on sitting here until I get it. *(Sits down)* You'll pay the day after tomorrow? I'll sit like this until the day after tomorrow. Here's how I'll sit. I ask you: do I have to pay interest tomorrow or not? Or do you think I'm joking?!

ELENA: I beg you to stop shouting. This is not a horse's stable.

GRIGORY: I'm not asking you about a horse's stable, but about—do I have to pay interest tomorrow or not?

ELENA: You don't know how to behave in women's company.

GRIGORY: No, ma'am, I do know how to behave in women's company.

ELENA: You're a crude, ill-bred person. Decent people don't talk to women like this.

GRIGORY: How would you have me talk to you? In French, maybe? *(Lisps angrily)* Madame, zhe voo pree...' how happy I am that you're not paying me my money. Ah, pardon that I've troubled you. Such lovely weather today.

ELENA: Stupid and crude.

GRIGORY: *(Imitating her)* Stupid and crude. I don't know how to behave in women's company. I've seen far more women in my life, madam, than you've seen sparrows. I've fought three duels over women, I've left twelve women, nine have left me. There was a time when I played the fool, cozied up, honey-tongued, cast pearls, bowed and scraped. I loved, suffered, sighed under the moon, went soft, melted, turned cold. I loved passionately, wildly, in every possible way, chattered like a magpie about women's rights, spent half my fortune on tender feelings, but now—I won't be taken in. Enough. "Dark eyes, passionate eyes," red lips, dimpled cheeks, the moon, whispers, timid sighs—I wouldn't give a cent for any of it, madam. Present company excepted, all women, big and small, are affected, mincing gossips, full of hate, liars to the marrow of their bones, fussy, petty, pitiless, with outrageous logic, and as for up here *(slaps his forehead)*—forgive me my frankness—a sparrow's a far better philosopher than these skirts.

You look at one of these poetic creatures: lace, perfume, a million raptures, but look into her soul—a most ordinary crocodile. But most outrageous of all is that this crocodile for some reason imagines that tender feelings are its chef-d'oeuvre, its privilege and monopoly. God damn me and hang me upside down on a nail—can a woman love anyone except her lapdog? All she can do in love is whimper and snivel. Where a man suffers and sacrifices, all she can do to express her love is swirl her skirts around and try to grab him fast by the nose. You have the misfortune to be a woman, so you know a woman's nature from your own self. Tell me honestly: have you ever in your life seen a woman who could be sincere, faithful, and constant? You'll sooner meet a cat with horns or a white woodcock than a constant woman.

ELENA: Excuse me, but who then, in your opinion, is faithful and constant in love? The man?

GRIGORY: Yes, ma'am, the man.

ELENA: The man. A man faithful and constant in love. That's quite some news. Men—faithful and constant. While we're at it, I'll tell you that, of all the men I've known and know now, the best was my late husband. I loved him passionately, with my whole being, as only a young, thinking woman can love; I gave him my youth, my happiness, my life, my fortune; I doted on him, I worshipped him like a pagan, and... and—what then? This best of men deceived me most unscrupulously at every step. After his death I found in his desk a whole drawer full of love letters, and while he was alive—it's terrible to remember —he left me on my own for weeks at a time, he courted other women and betrayed me before my very eyes, he squandered my money, he made a joke of my feelings. And, despite all that, I loved him and was faithful to him. What's more, he died, and I'm still faithful to him and constant. I've buried myself forever within these four walls and till my grave I will never stop mourning.

GRIGORY: Mourning. What do you take me for? As if I don't understand why you wear this black domino and have buried yourself within these four walls. It's so mysterious, so poetic. Some junior officer or paltry poet will drive past your house, look at the windows, and think: "Here lives that mysterious widow, who has buried herself within four walls out of love for her husband." We know these tricks.

ELENA: How dare you say all that to me.

GRIGORY: You've buried yourself alive, but you haven't forgotten to powder your nose.

ELENA: How dare you speak to me like that?!

GRIGORY: Don't shout, I'm not your servant.

ELENA: I'm not shouting, you are! Kindly leave me in peace.

GRIGORY: Give me the money and I'll go.

ELENA: Just to spite you, I won't give you a cent. Now leave me in peace.

He sits down.

So you just sit down?

(calls) Luka!

(to Grigory) I ask you to leave. I have no wish to talk with louts. Kindly get out of here. You won't get out?

LUKA enters.

Luka, show this gentleman out.

LUKA: Sir, kindly leave when you're told. There's nothing for you here...

GRIGORY: Shut up. Who do you think you're talking to? I'll chop you to pieces.

ELENA: Where's Dasha? Dasha!
(Shouts) Dasha! Pelágeya! Dasha!

LUKA: They've all gone out berry picking. Nobody's home.

ELENA: Kindly get out of here!

GRIGORY: Would you mind being more polite?

ELENA: You're a clod! A crude bear. An oaf. A monster.

GRIGORY: What? What did you say?

ELENA: I said you're a bear, a monster.

GRIGORY: What right do you have to insult me?

ELENA: So I'm insulting you. What of it? Do you think I'm afraid of you?

GRIGORY: You think that if you're a poetic creature you have the right to insult me with impunity? I challenge you!

LUKA: Oh God...

GRIGORY: A duel...

ELENA: Just because you've got big fists and a bull's neck, you think I'm afraid of you? An oaf!

GRIGORY: I challenge you. I won't allow anyone to insult me, and I don't care if you're a woman, a weak creature.

ELENA: A bear. A bear. A bear.

GRIGORY: It's time at last to get rid of the prejudice that only men should pay for their insults. Equal rights are equal rights, God damn it. I challenge you.

ELENA: A duel, is it? Very well.

GRIGORY: This minute.

ELENA: This minute. My husband left behind some pistols . . . I'll go get them... What a pleasure it will be to plant a bullet in your thick skull! *(Exits)*

GRIGORY: I'll gun her down like a chicken. I'm not a little boy, not a sentimental puppy, for me there aren't any weak creatures.

LUKA: Young fellow, go away.

GRIGORY: A duel—that's equality, women's rights. Here the two sexes are equal. I'll shoot her on principle.

LUKA: Go away... Please, go away.

He exits.

GRIGORY: *(Imitating)* "I'll plant a bullet in your thick skull..."

Pause.

She's red in the face, her eyes flash. She accepted my challenge. That's something. Honest to God, this is the first time I've seen such a woman. Quite something. A real woman. Not a whimperer, a namby-pamby, but fire, gunpowder, a rocket. I'll even be sorry to kill her.

Pause.

I like her. I do. My anger is gone. Maybe I could forgive her the debt... An astonishing woman. Even though she has dimples.

ELENA: *(Enters with pistols)* Here are the pistols... But before we fight, kindly show me how to shoot. I've never held a pistol in my life.

GRIGORY: *(Looking over the pistols)* You see, there are several kinds of pistols... There's the special Mortimer caplock duelling pistol. But yours are Smith and Wesson revolvers, triple-lock with extractor and central sight. Excellent pistols. They cost ninety rubles a pair, at a minimum. You must hold the pistol like this.

ELENA: Like this?

GRIGORY: Yes, like that. Then you cock it . Aim it like this. Head slightly back. Hold your arm out straight. Like this. Then you press this little thing with this finger—and that's it. Only the main rule is: don't get excited and don't hurry when you aim. Make sure your hand doesn't jerk.

ELENA: Very good. You don't shoot inside, let's go to the garden.

GRIGORY: Yes, let's. Only I warn you that I'm going to fire into the air.

ELENA: Why?

GRIGORY: Because...

ELENA: You're turning coward? Is that it? No, sir, don't you wriggle out of it. Kindly follow me. I won't calm down till I've put a hole in this head of yours. This head I hate so much. Are you turning coward?

GRIGORY: Yes, I am.

ELENA: Liar. Why don't you want to fight?

GRIGORY: Listen. Are you still angry? I'm also damned furious, but, you see. How shall I put it? You see, there's this thing, this, sort of, as a matter of fact. Well, so, is it my fault that I like you? I like you..

ELENA: You like me... You dare to tell me you like me. Please. Go away—I hate you.

GRIGORY: Never in my life have I seen the likes of you. Your eyes, there's fire in them. I'm lost. A mouse in a trap.

ELENA: Go away or I'll shoot.

GRIGORY: Shoot. I've lost my mind. I'm a nobleman, a decent person, I have an income of ten thousand a year. Can put a bullet through a tossed coin. Own excellent horses.

ELENA: *(shakes her pistol at him)* I challenge you. I'll shoot you.

GRIGORY: Shoot. To be shot by a pistol held by that small, velvet hand. I've left twelve women, nine have left me. I've gone weak, soft, melted away. Shame and disgrace. I haven't fallen in love for five years, I vowed not to. Yes or no? You don't want to? Never mind.

ELENA: Wait. Never mind, go. No, wait. No, go, go! I hate you. Or no. Don't go. If you only knew how angry, how angry I am. *(Sets the pistol on the table)* My fingers are swollen from holding that disgusting thing. Why are you standing there? Get out.

GRIGORY: Goodbye.

ELENA: Yes, yes, go.. Where are you going? Wait.

(shouts) Luka!

No, get out. I am so angry. Don't come near me.

GRIGORY: I'm so angry with myself.

LUKA enters.

ELENA: *(to LUKA)* Tell them in the stables not to give Toby any oats today.

LUKA exits.

(to GRIGORY) I hate you. I challenge you. Get out. Wait! I'm so angry!

GRIGORY: Me too...

LIGHTS FADE.

CHARACTERS

STEPÁN STEPÁNOVICH CHUBUKOV
a landowner

NATÁLYA STEPÁNOVNA
his daughter, age twenty-five

IVÁN VASSÍLYEVICH LÓMOV
Stepan's neighboring landowner, a hale hypochondriac

A PROPOSAL

The action takes place on STEPAN's estate.

A room in STEPAN's house.

IVAN, well dressed, sits waiting.

STEPAN: *(entering)* Who's this I see. Ivan Vassilyevich. Very glad. This is really a surprise, sonny boy. How are you doing?

IVAN: Well, thank you. And how might you be doing?

STEPAN: A bit at a time, my angel, by your prayers and all that. Sit down. It's really not nice to forget your neighbors. Why this attire? Are you going somewhere, my good lad?

IVAN: No, only to you, Stepan.

STEPAN: Why dressed like this, then, my dear friend? As if it's a New Year's visit.

IVAN: You see, here's the thing. I've come to you, Stepan, to trouble you with a request. It's more than once that I've had the honor of asking for your help, and you've always, so to speak, but, excuse me, I'm nervous. May I have some water? I'm terribly nervous, as you can see. In short, you alone are able to help me, though, of course, I don't deserve it at all and... and have no right to count on your help.

STEPAN: Don't smear it around. Say it straight out. Well?

IVAN: Right away. This very moment. The thing is that I've come to ask for the hand of your daughter Natalya.

STEPAN: My boy... Ivan Vassilyevich! Say it again—I want to hear it again.

IVAN: I have the honor...

STEPAN: My dear chum, I'm so glad and all that. Positively and so forth. I've long wanted it. It has been my constant wish. I've always loved you, my angel, like my own son. God grant both of you love and harmony and all that, and I greatly wish... Why am I sitting here like a blockhead? I'm flabbergasted, completely flabbergasted. With all my heart, I... I'll go call Natasha and so forth.

IVAN: Do you think I can count on her acceptance, Stepan?

STEPAN: You, such a handsome fellow—and... and how could she not accept? She's sure to be madly in love and all that. *(Exits)*

IVAN: *(Alone)* It's cold. I'm trembling, like before an exam. Be resolute —that's the main thing. If you think for too long, hesitate, talk too much, wait for an ideal or perfect love, you'll never get married. It's cold. Natalya will be an excellent housewife, not bad-looking, educated. What more do I need? I'm already getting a humming in my ears from nervousness. I can't not get married. First of all, I'm already thirty-five years old—a critical age, so they say. Second of all, I need a proper, regular life. I have a weak heart, constant palpitations, anxious and always terribly nervous. Right now my lips are trembling and there's a twitching in my right eyelid. But the worst thing for me is sleep. As soon as I lie down in bed and just begin to fall asleep, something goes—stab!—in my left side, and it hits me right in the shoulder and in the head. I jump up like a madman, walk around a little, and lie down again, but just as I begin to fall asleep, again it goes—stab!—in my side. And it does it maybe twenty times.

NATALYA: *(Enters)* So it's you. And papa says: go, there's a merchant who's come for his goods. Greetings, Ivan.

IVAN: Greetings, Natalya!

NATALYA: Excuse my apron. We're shelling peas for drying. Why haven't you come for so long? Sit down.

(They sit down.)

Would you like something to eat?

IVAN: No thank you, I've already eaten.

NATALYA: You can smoke. Here are some matches. Splendid weather, but yesterday there was such rain that the workers did nothing all day. How many haystacks have you mowed? I, just imagine, got greedy and had the whole meadow mowed, but now I regret it, I'm afraid all my hay will rot. It would have been better to wait. But what's this? Why are you dressed up? Are you going to a party or something? By the way, you've grown quite handsome. No, really, why are you so dressed up?

IVAN: You see, Natalya. The thing is, I've resolved to ask you to hear me out. Of course, you'll be surprised and even angry, but I...

NATALYA: What's this about?Well?

IVAN: You are aware, that I have had the honor of knowing your family for a long time now, ever since childhood. My late aunt and her spouse, from whom, as you are pleased to know, I inherited my land, always had the profoundest respect for your father and your late mother. The families of the Lomovs and the Chubukovs always maintained the most cordial and, one might even say, familial relations. Besides, as you are pleased to know, my land is closely contiguous with yours. If you will be pleased to recall, my Oxen Meadows border on your birch grove.

NATALYA: Excuse me for interrupting you. You say "my Oxen Meadows". You think they're yours?

IVAN: Yes, ma'am . . .

NATALYA: The Oxen Meadows are ours, not yours.

IVAN: No, ma'am, they're mine, Natalya.

NATALYA: That's news to me. How are they yours?

IVAN: What do you mean, "how"? I'm talking about the Oxen Meadows that form a wedge between your birch grove and Burnt Swamp.

NATALYA: Yes, yes. They're ours.

IVAN: No, you're mistaken, Natalya.

NATALYA: Come to your senses, Ivan. Since when have they been yours?

IVAN: As far back as I can remember, they've always been ours.

NATALYA: Well, sorry, but that's...

IVAN: It's clear from the documents, Natalya. The Oxen Meadows used to be contested—it's true; but now it's known to everybody that they're mine. And there's no point arguing about it. Kindly understand, my aunt's grandmother gave these Meadows to your father's grandfather's peasants for free use in perpetuity in exchange for baking bricks for her. Your father's grandfather's peasants had free use of the Meadows for about forty years and they just got accustomed to considering them their own.

NATALYA: It's not at all as you say. Both my grandfather and great-grandfather considered that their land extended as far as Burnt Swamp—meaning that the Oxen Meadows were ours. What's there to argue about? I don't understand.

IVAN: I'll show you the documents, Natalya.

NATALYA: You're simply joking or teasing. We've owned this land for some three hundred years, and suddenly we're informed that the land isn't ours. Forgive me, Ivan, but I can't even believe my

ears. Those Meadows aren't dear to me. There are just fifteen acres in all, worth only about 300 rubles, but I'm outraged by injustice. Say what you like, but I can't bear injustice.

IVAN: Your father's grandfather's peasants, as I've already had the honor of telling you, baked bricks for my aunt's grandmother. My aunt's grandmother, wishing to be nice to them . . .

NATALYA: Grandfather, grandmother, aunt... I don't understand any of it. The Meadows are ours, that's it.

IVAN: Mine, ma'am.

NATALYA: Ours. Spend two days proving it, put on fifteen ties, but they're ours, ours, ours. I want nothing of yours and I don't want to lose what's ours. Say what you like.

IVAN: Me, Natalya, I don't need the Meadows, but I have principles. If it suits you, fine, I'll give them to you.

NATALYA: I myself can give them to you, they're mine. This is all very strange to say the least, Ivan. Up to now we've considered you a good neighbor, a friend; last year we lent you our thresher, on account of which we had to finish our own threshing in November; but you treat us as if we're crooks. You give me my own land. Sorry, but that's not neighborly. In my opinion, it's even insolent, if you like.

IVAN: So in your view I come out as a usurper? My good lady, I have never seized other people's land, and I will not allow anyone to accuse me of it. *(Drinks some water)* The Oxen Meadows are mine.

NATALYA: No, they're ours. I'll prove it to you. Today I'll send my mowers to those Meadows.

IVAN: What's that?

NATALYA: Today my mowers will be there.

IVAN: And I'll kick them out.

NATALYA: You wouldn't dare.

IVAN: *(Clutches his heart)* The Oxen Meadows are mine. Understand?!

NATALYA: Please don't shout. You can shout and choke with rage in your own home, but here I ask you to restrain yourself.

IVAN: If it weren't for this terrible pounding of my heart, if it weren't for the blood throbbing in my temples, I would speak differently with you. *(Shouts)* The Oxen Meadows are mine!

NATALYA: Ours.

IVAN: Mine.

NATALYA: Ours.

IVAN: Mine.

STEPAN: *(Enters)* What's going on? Why the shouting?

NATALYA: Papa, please explain to this gentleman who the Oxen Meadows belong to: us or him?

STEPAN: *(To IVAN)* The Meadows are ours, my pet.

IVAN: I beg your pardon, Stepan, what makes them yours? You at least be a reasonable man. My aunt's grandmother gave the Meadows to your grandfather's peasants for temporary, free use. The peasants made use of the land for forty years and got accustomed to it as if it was theirs.

STEPAN: You're forgetting that the peasants weren't paying your grandmother and all that precisely because the Meadows were in dispute then and so forth. But now every local dog knows, precisely, that they're ours. It means you haven't seen the map.

IVAN: I'll prove to you that they're mine.

STEPAN: You won't prove it, my dearest.

IVAN: I will prove it.

STEPAN: I don't want what's yours, and I don't intend to lose what's mine. Why on earth should I? If it goes so far, my chum, that you want to dispute about the Meadows and all that, then I'd sooner give them to the peasants than to you. So there.

IVAN: What right do you have to give away someone else's property?

STEPAN: Allow me to decide whether I have the right or not. Precisely, young man, I'm not used to being talked to in such a tone and all that. I'm twice your age, young man, and I ask you to speak to me without agitation and so forth.

IVAN: You simply take me for a fool and are laughing at me. You call my land yours, and you also want me to remain cool and speak with you like a human being. Good neighbors don't behave that way, Stepan. You're not a neighbor, you're a usurper.

STEPAN: What did you say?

NATALYA: Papa, send mowers to the Meadows right now.

STEPAN: *(To IVAN)* What did you say, my dear sir?

NATALYA: The Oxen Meadows are ours, and I won't give in, I won't, I won't.

IVAN: We'll see about that... I'll prove to you in court that they're mine.

STEPAN: You can go to court, my dear sir, and so forth. You can. I know you, all you do is precisely wait for an occasion to go to court and all that. A finagler. Your family were all litigious. All of them.

IVAN: I ask you not to insult my family. The Lomov family were all honest, and not one of them was taken to court for embezzlement like your uncle!

STEPAN: And you Lomovs were all madmen.

NATALYA: All, all, all...

STEPAN: Your grandfather drank like a fish, and your younger aunt, Nastasya, precisely eloped with a contractor and all that.

IVAN: Your mother was lopsided. *(Clutches his heart)* A stabbing in my side.

STEPAN: Your father was a gambler and a glutton.

NATALYA: It's hard to find a gossip to match your aunt!

IVAN: My left leg's gone numb. And you're a schemer. And it's no secret from anybody that before the election you went... There are sparks in my eyes. Where's my hat?

NATALYA: Low. Dishonest. Vile.

STEPAN: You yourself are precisely a nasty, two-faced conniver.

IVAN: My hat... My heart. I think I'm dying. *(He goes)*

STEPAN: And don't set foot in my house again.

NATALYA: Go to court. We'll see.

STEPAN: To hell with him.

NATALYA: Go trusting good neighbors after that.

STEPAN: A villain. A scarecrow.

NATALYA: Ugly mug. Appropriates people's land, and then dares to insult them.

STEPAN: And this troll, this dimwit precisely dares to come with a proposal and all that. With a proposal.

NATALYA: What sort of proposal?

STEPAN: He came to propose to you.

NATALYA: To propose? To me?

STEPAN: That's why he got dressed up. A sausage. A pipsqueak.

NATALYA: To me? To propose? Bring him back. Bring him back. Oh no. Bring him back.

STEPAN: Bring who back?

NATALYA: Quickly. I feel sick. Bring him back.

STEPAN: What's the matter?

NATALYA: I'm dying. Bring him back. *(STEPAN Runs off)* *(Alone)* I'm sick. What have we done? Bring him back, please.

STEPAN: (*Returns*) He'll come right away and all that, to hell with him. Talk to him yourself, I precisely don't want to.

NATALYA: Bring him back.

STEPAN: He's coming. What a chore to be the father of a grown-up daughter. I'll kill myself. I'll definitely kill myself. We abused him, disgraced him, drove him out, and it's all you... you.

NATALYA: No, it's you.

STEPAN: So I'm the guilty one, precisely.

(IVAN appears.)

Talk to him yourself. *(Exits)*

IVAN: *(Enters)* My leg's gone numb. There's a stabbing in my side.

NATALYA: Forgive me, we got too excited, Ivan. I remember now: the Oxen Meadows are actually yours.

IVAN: My heart's pounding. I've got a twitching in both eyelids...

NATALYA: Yours, the Meadows are yours. Sit down.

(They sit down.)

We were wrong.

IVAN: It's a matter of principle. I don't care about the land, I care about the principle.

NATALYA: Precisely the principle. Let's talk about something else.

IVAN: All the more so in that I have proof. My aunt's grandmother gave your father's grandfather's—

NATALYA: Enough, enough of that. Do you plan to go hunting soon?

IVAN: For black grouse, Natalya, I think we'll begin after the harvest. Oh, have you heard? My dog Spotter, whom you're pleased to know, has gone lame.

NATALYA: What a pity. How did it happen?

IVAN: I don't know. Must be he dislocated it, or some other dog bit him. He's my best dog, not to mention the cost. I paid a hundred and twenty-five rubles for him.

NATALYA: That's far too much, Ivan.

IVAN: In my opinion it's very cheap. He's a wonderful dog.

NATALYA: Papa paid eighty-five rubles for his Swifty, and Swifty is ever so much better than your Spotter.

IVAN: Swifty better than Spotter? *(Laughs)* Swifty better than Spotter.

NATALYA: Swifty's young, true, he's not mature yet, but in terms of temperament and conformation, he's even better than any of Volchanétsky's dogs.

IVAN: Excuse me, Natalya, but you're forgetting that he has an overshot jaw, and such dogs are always poor retrievers.

NATALYA: Overshot jaw? It's the first I hear of it.

IVAN: I assure you, his lower jaw is shorter than the upper.

NATALYA: You've measured it?

IVAN: Yes, I've measured it. He's fine for the chase, but for the catch...

NATALYA: Our Swifty is a purebred, thick-coated borzoi, he's the son of Strapper and Chisel, and you'll never dig up the breed of your blotchy piebald. Besides, he's old and ugly as a worn-out rag.

IVAN: He may be old, but I wouldn't take five of your Swiftys for him. Spotter's a dog, while Swifty... it's even ridiculous to argue. Every whipper-in has dogs like your Swifty—up to here! Twenty- five rubles is the top price.

NATALYA: Some demon is sitting in you today, Ivan, contradicting everything. First you think up that the Oxen Meadows are yours, now that Spotter's better than Swifty. I hate it when a person says what he doesn't think. You know perfectly well that Swifty is a hundred times better than your... this stupid Spotter. Why do you say the contrary?

IVAN: I can see, Natalya, that you think I'm blind, or a fool. Try to understand that your Swifty has an overshot jaw.

NATALYA: Not true.

IVAN: Overshot.

NATALYA: And it's time your Spotter was put down.

IVAN: I'm having palpitations.

NATALYA: I've noticed that the hunters who argue the most understand the least.

IVAN: Please, be quiet. Be quiet.

NATALYA: I won't be quiet, as long as you don't admit that Swifty is a hundred times better than your Spotter!

IVAN: He's a hundred times worse. I wish he'd drop dead, your Swifty.

NATALYA: Your idiotic Spotter has no need to drop dead, because he's dead already.

IVAN: Quiet. I'm having a heart attack.

NATALYA: I won't be quiet.

STEPAN: *(Enters)* What's going on?

NATALYA: Papa, tell us frankly, in all honesty: which dog is better —our Swifty or his Spotter?

IVAN: Stepan, I beg you, say just one thing: does your Swifty have an overshot jaw or not? Yes or no?

STEPAN: What if he does? Big deal. There's no better dog in the whole district and all that.

IVAN: But isn't my Spotter better? Honestly.

STEPAN: Your Spotter precisely has his good qualities. He's purebred, has sturdy legs, steep haunches, and so forth. But this same dog, if you want to know, has two essential shortcomings: he's old, and he has a blunt snout.

IVAN: I'm having palpitations. Let's consider the facts. In Maruska's field my Spotter ran ear to ear with the count's Swinger, and your Swifty lagged a whole mile behind.

STEPAN: He lagged behind because the count's whipper-in lashed him with his whip.

IVAN: For good reason. All the dogs went after a fox, Swifty started worrying a sheep.

STEPAN: Not true, sir. He lashed him because everyone was looking at my dog with envy. Everybody's full of hate. And you, sir, are not without sin. As soon as you precisely notice that someone's dog is better than your Spotter, right away you start... That same thing... and so forth...

IVAN: My leg's gone numb.

NATALYA: (*Teases him*) Palpitations. What kind of hunter are you? You should lie by the stove in the kitchen and squash cockroaches, and not go chasing after foxes. Palpitations.

STEPAN: What kind of hunter are you? With your palpitations.

IVAN: And you're a hunter, are you? You only go hunting to butter up the count. You're a brown noser.

STEPAN: Me, a brown noser? Don't...

IVAN: Brown noser.

STEPAN: Milksop. Puppy.

IVAN: Old rat. Jesuit.

STEPAN: Be quiet, or I'll fire my dirty shotgun at you like a partridge. You twit.

IVAN: Everybody knows that your late wife used to beat you. My foot. Temples. Sparks.

STEPAN: You're under your housekeeper's thumb.

IVAN: My heart just burst. Where's my shoulder? *(Collapses in an armchair) Doctor... (Passes out.)*

STEPAN: Milksop. Puppy. Twit. Fainted.

NATALYA: What kind of hunter are you? You can't even seat a horse. *(To her father)* What's the matter with him? Papa, look. Ivan Vassilyevich. He's dead. *(Tugs at Ivan's tie)* Ivan Vassilyevich. What have we done? He's dead.

STEPAN: What is this? What's the matter with you?

NATALYA: He's dead ... dead.

STEPAN: *(Puts a glass to Ivan's mouth)* Drink. He doesn't drink. Means he's dead and so forth. Why don't I put a bullet through my head? Why didn't I cut my throat long ago? Give me a knife. Give me a pistol.

(IVAN stirs.)

He's reviving . Drink some water. That's it...

IVAN: Sparks. Fog. Where am I?

STEPAN: She accepts! She accepts and so forth. I bless you and all that.

IVAN: Who? What?

STEPAN: She accepts! Kiss and... and the devil take both of you!

(He goes.)

NATALYA: Yes, yes, I accept...

IVAN: Who? What?

NATALYA: And I'm happy...

LIGHTS FADE.

CHARACTERS

EVDOKÍM ZAKHÁROVICH ZHIGÁLOV
a minor civil servant, retired

NASTÁSYA TIMOFÉEVNA
his wife

DÁSHENKA
their daughter

EPAMINÓND MAXÍMOVICH APLÓMBOV
her fiancé

FYÓDOR YÁKOVLEVICH REVUNÓV-KARAÚLOV
second-class captain, retired

ANDRÉI ANDRÉEVICH NIÚNIN
insurance agent

ÁNNA MARTÍNOVNA ZMEYÚKINA
midwife, 30 years old, in bright crimson dress

IVÁN MIKHÁILOVICH ZED
telegrapher

KHARLÁMPY SPIRIDÓNOVICH DYMBA
Greek confectioner

THE WEDDING

ZHIGÁLOV home. A table set with food, a supper.

NASTÁSYA looks over the table and food; with APLÓMBOV and DÁSHENKA.

NASTÁSYA: Why are you bothering me with all sorts of words?

APLÓMBOV: Pardon me, dear Mama, but there is so much I don't understand in your behavior. For instance, besides objects of household utility, you promised to give me a zinc tub along with your daughter. Where is it?

NASTÁSYA: I'm getting a headache. Must be bad weather's coming on. There'll be a thaw.

APLÓMBOV: Don't give me a runaround. I learned today that your zinc tub has been pawned. Pardon me, dear Mama, but only exploiters behave that way. I'm not saying it out of egotism —but out of principle, and I won't allow anybody to cheat me. I've made your daughter's happiness, but if you don't give me the tub, I'll turn her life into mush. I am an honorable man.

NASTÁSYA: *(Looking over the food and counting the plates)* One, two, three, four, five...

APLÓMBOV: And you also promised, and an agreement was reached, that there would be a general at tonight's wedding supper. And where is he, may I ask?

NASTÁSYA: That, my dear man, is not my fault.

APLÓMBOV: Then whose is it?

NASTÁSYA: Niunin's. He came yesterday and promised to bring a most genuine general. Must be he didn't find one anywhere, otherwise he'd have brought him. Have we begrudged you anything? For our own child we won't begrudge anything.

APLÓMBOV: To continue... Everybody, including you, dear Mama, knows that before I proposed to Dashenka, she was being courted by this telegrapher Zed. Why did you invite him? Didn't you know I'd find it unpleasant?

NASTÁSYA: Epaminónd, you're not even married a day and you've already worn me and Dashenka out with all your talk. How will it be in a year? What a bore you are.

She goes off.

DÁSHENKA: So she doesn't like hearing the truth.

APLÓMBOV: She should behave honorably. I want only one thing from her: be honorable.

ZED and ZMEYÚKINA enter.

ZED: *(To ZMEYÚKINA)* Have a heart.

ZMEYÚKINA: I told you already, I'm not in voice today.

ZED: Sing, I beg you. Just one note. Have a heart. One note.

ZMEYÚKINA: I'm sick of you.

ZED: You're simply merciless. Such a cruel creature, if you'll allow me to say so, and such a wonderful, wonderful voice. With such a voice, if you'll pardon the expression, you should be singing at public concerts, not working as a midwife. For instance, how divinely you produce this fioritura... this one... *(Sings)* "I loved you, loved you all in vain..."

ZMEYÚKINA: *(Sings)* "I loved you, love may still..." That one?

ZED: That's it exactly. Wonderful.

ZMEYÚKINA: I'm not in voice today. It's hot. *(To APLÓMBOV)* Why this melancholy? Can a bridegroom be like that? Shame on you. What are you brooding about?

APLÓMBOV: Marriage is a serious step. Everything has to be thought over comprehensively, thoroughly.

ZMEYÚKINA: What disgusting sceptics you all are. I suffocate around you. Give me atmosphere. Do you hear? Give me atmosphere. *(Sings)*

ZED: Wonderful.

ZMEYÚKINA: Fan me, I feel I'm about to have a heart attack. Tell me, please, why do I feel so stifled?

ZED: You're sweating.

ZMEYÚKINA: How vulgar you are. Don't you dare say such things.

ZED: Of course, you're used to aristocratic company, if you'll pardon the expression, and...

ZMEYÚKINA: Shut up. Leave me alone. Give me poetry, raptures. Fan me.

ZHIGÁLOV: *(enters with DYMBA)* Let's have another, shall we? One can drink anytime. The main thing, is not to forget what you're about. *(pours)* Drink, but also think. And if it comes to drinking, why not drink? One can always drink. Do you have tigers in Greece?

DYMBA: Yes.

ZHIGÁLOV: And lions?

DYMBA: Lion's, too. It's in Russia there's nothing, but in Greece there's everything. I've got a father there, and an uncle, and brothers, but here I've got nothing.

NASTÁSYA: *(entering)* Why all this drinking? It's time we sat down. Don't start on the meat balls. They're set aside for the general. He may still come.

ZHIGÁLOV: Do you eat meat balls in Greece?

DYMBA: Yes. We eat everything there.

ZHIGÁLOV: And are there civil servants?

ZMEYÚKINA: Greece. I can imagine what the atmosphere is like in Greece.

ZHIGÁLOV: And there must be a lot of swindling. Greeks are the same as Armenians or Gypsies. He sells you a sponge or a goldfish, but all he thinks about is ripping you off. Let's have another, shall we?

NASTÁSYA: Why another? It's time we all sat down. It's late.

ZHIGALOV: So let's sit then. Ladies and gentlemen, I humbly invite you. If you please. Supper. Young people...

NASTÁSYA: Dear guests, please be seated.

ZMEYÚKINA: Give me poetry. "And he, rebellious, seeks the storm,/ As if in storms he will find peace." Give me a storm...

ZED: Ladies and gentlemen. I must tell you the following. We have a great many toasts and speeches prepared. We won't wait, we'll begin at once. Ladies and gentlemen, I invite you to drink a toast to the newlyweds.

As they serve themselves. Few have sat down.

Cheers!

ALL: Cheers! Cheers!

APLÓMBOV and DÁSHENKA kiss.

ZHIGÁLOV: And are there sperm whales in Greece?

DYMBA: There's everything.

ZED: Wonderful. Wonderful. I must express to you, ladies and gentlemen, and I say it in all impartiality, that this home and the space here in general is magnificent. Splendid, charming. Only do you know what's lacking to complete the festivities? Electric light, if you'll pardon the expression. Electric light has already been introduced in all countries, and Russia alone lags behind.

ZHIGÁLOV: Electricity. And in my opinion, electric light is nothing but a swindle. They slip in a bit of carbon and think they can hoodwink us. No, brother, if you're going to give us light, don't give us a bit of carbon, give us something substantial, something distinctive, so that we can take hold of it. Give us fire—understand?—fire, that's natural and not mental.

ZED: If you had ever seen an electric battery, and what it's made of, you'd reason differently.

ZHIGÁLOV: I have no wish to see one. Swindling. They hoodwink simple people. Squeeze the last drop out of them. We know them, those... And you, my young sir, instead of sticking up for swindling, would do better to drink and pour for the others.

APLÓMBOV: I agree with Papa. Why start learned conversations? I myself am not against talking about all sorts of discoveries in the scientific line, but this is not the time for it. *(To DÁSHENKA)* What do you think, *mashair*?

DÁSHENKA: Mr. Zed wants to show his *education* and always talks about what nobody understands.

NASTÁSYA: Thank God, we've lived our life without education, and she's the third daughter we're marrying to a good man.

And if, in your opinion, we walk around uneducated, then why do you call on us?

Go to your educated ones.

ZED: I have always respected your family, Nastásya, and if I have a thing about electric light, it doesn't mean I'm proud. Look, I'll drink to you. With all my heart, I've always wished Dáshenka a happy marriage. In our time, Nastásya, it's hard to find a good man to marry. Nowadays everybody aims to marry for convenience, for money.

APLÓMBOV: What are you hinting at?

ZED: I'm not talking about the present company. I meant it just... generally. For goodness' sake. Everyone knows you're doing it out of love. The dowry's piddling.

NASTÁSYA: It's not piddling. Don't let your tongue run away with you, sir. Besides a thousand rubles in cash, we're giving three overcoats, bed linen, and all the furniture. Try finding such a dowry anywhere else.

ZED: I didn't mean... The furniture's really good and... and the overcoats, too, of course. What I meant was that he's offended at my hinting.

NASTÁSYA: Don't hint, then. We respect you on account of your parents, so we invited you to the wedding, and then there's all these words. And if you knew that Epaminónd was marrying for convenience, why were you silent till now? I nursed her, nourished her, nurtured her. Cherished her more than an emerald diamond, my little baby.

APLÓMBOV: Then you believe him? I humbly thank you. Thank you very much.

DÁSHENKA: *(To her mother)* Mama, are you upset? I'm happy.

APLÓMBOV: Mama is upset about the coming separation. But I would advise her that she would do better to remember our recent conversation. *(To ZED)* And you, Mister Zed, though you're my acquaintance, I will not allow you to perform such outrages in someone else's house. Kindly clear out.

ZED: How's that?

APLOMBOV: I wish you were as honorable a man as I am. In short, kindly clear out.

ZHIGÁLOV: *(To APLÓMBOV)* Let him be. Enough. Is it worth it? Sit down.

ZED: Never mind. I just... I don't even understand. If you wish, I'll leave. Only first pay me back the five rubles you borrowed last year to buy a *piqué* waistcoat, pardon the expression. I'll have another drink and... and leave, only first pay back what you owe.

ZHIGÁLOV: Enough, enough now. No more. Is it worth quarreling over trifles?

DÁSHENKA: *(to APLÓMBOV)* Sit down.

ZED: To the health of the bride's parents.

NASTÁSYA: Speech... Speech!

ZHIGÁLOV: *(stands)* Thank you. Dear guests. Thank you very much for not forgetting us and joining us, for not scorning us. And for not thinking I was some sort of rascal or up to some swindling on my side, I'm simply moved. From the bottom of my heart. I won't spare anything for good people. My humble thanks. *(sits)* Are there oyster mushrooms in Greece?

DYMBA: Yes. There's everything.

ZHIGÁLOV: But certainly not black trumpets.

DYMBA: Black trumpets, too. There's everything.

ZED: Kharlámpy, it's your turn to give a speech. Ladies and gentlemen, let him make a speech.

ALL: *(To DYMBA)* Speech! Speech! It's your turn!

DYMBA: Why? I don't understand. What is this?

ZMEYÚKINA: Don't you dare refuse. It's your turn. Stand up!

DYMBA: *(Stands up)* I can speak this... There is Russia and there is Greece. Now there are people in Russia and people in Greece. And we sail over the sea in caravels, which in Russian means boats, and you go over the land which are called railroads. I understand very well. We are Greeks, you are Russians, and I need nothing. I can speak this... there is Russia and there is Greece.

Enter NIÚNIN

NIÚNIN: Ladies and gentlemen, don't start eating! Nastásya, one moment. *(to NASTÁSYA)*. A general is coming right now. I finally found one. I'm exhausted. A real general, a distinguished one, old, maybe eighty, or even ninety.

NASTÁSYA: When is he coming?

NIÚNIN: This minute. You'll be grateful for the rest of your life. He's a real plum. Not some sort of foot- soldier, not an infantryman, but from the navy. In rank he's a second-class captain, but in their terms, in the navy, that's the same as a major general, or an actual state councilor in the civil service. It's decidedly the same. Even higher.

NASTÁSYA: You're not deceiving me, Andrei dear?

NIÚNIN: Am I a crook or something?

NASTÁSYA: I don't want to waste money, Andrei dear.

NIÚNIN: He's not just a general, he's a picture. So I say to him: "You've forgotten us, Your Excellency. It's not nice, Your Excellency, to forget old acquaintances! Nastásya," I say, "has a big grudge against you!" And he says: "For pity's sake, my friend, how can I go if I'm not acquainted with the bridegroom?" "Oh, come now, Your Excellency, what's all this ceremony? The bridegroom," I say, "is a wonderful man, wears his heart on his sleeve. He works as an appraiser for a pawnbroker, but don't go thinking, Your Excellency, that he's some sort of ne'er-do-well or idle youth. Even noble ladies work for pawnbrokers nowadays."

APLÓMBOV: When is he coming?

NIÚNIN: Right now. He is taking off his galoshes... He slapped me on the shoulder, we each smoked a Havana cigar, and now he's coming.

Enter REVUNÓV-KARAÚLOV.

NASTÁSYA: Welcome, Your Excellency. We're so pleased.

REVUNÓV: Very.

ZHIGÁLOV: We, Your Excellency, are not noble people, not exalted people, we are simple people, but don't think there's any swindling on our part. For us, good people are foremost, we won't stint on anything. You're most welcome.

REVUNÓV: Very glad.

NIÚNIN: Your Excellency, allow me to make the introductions,. The bridegroom with his newly wedded wife. Zed, serving as a telegrapher. Kharlámpy, a foreigner of Greek rank who works in the pastry-cooking line. And so on and so forth.

NASTÁSYA: Sit down, Your Excellency. Be so kind. Eat. Only excuse us, you must be accustomed to delicacy, but with us it's all simple.

REVUNÓV: Yes, ma'am. In the old days people always lived simply and were content. I'm a man of a certain rank, but I, too, live simply. Today Andryusha comes to me and invites me to this wedding.
How can I go, I say, if I don't know them? It's awkward. And he says: "They're simple, patriarchal people, every guest makes them glad." Well, of course, in that case, why not? I'm very glad. It's boring for me at home alone, and if my presence at a wedding can give people pleasure, then I say do them the favor.

ZHIGÁLOV: So it's from the heart, Your Excellency? I respect that. I'm a simple man, without any swindling, and I respect such people. Help yourself, Your Excellency.

APLÓMBOV: Did you retire long ago, Your Excellency?

REVUNÓV: Yes, yes. That's true. But, excuse me, what's this, now? Salty... salty. Ah, here are the sweets... Yes, sir. In the old days everything was simple and everybody was content. I like simplicity. I'm an old man, I retired in one thousand eight hundred and sixty-five. I'm seventy- two. Yes. Of course, before, too, they didn't do without a bit of showing off on occasion, but... Any sailors here?

NIÚNIN: I don't think so.

REVUNÓV: Aha... So... Yes Naval service has always been difficult. There's something in it to ponder and rack your brains over. Every insignificant word has, so to speak, its special meaning. For example: foretopman to the main topgallant shroud. What does that mean? A sailor understands of course. It's subtler than your mathematics.

NIÚNIN: To the health of His Excellency.

ZED: Here's to you, Your Excellency. You have just been pleased to express yourself concerning the difficulty of naval service. But is telegraphy any easier? Nowadays, Your Excellency, no one can enter the telegraph service unless he's able to read and write in French and German. But the most difficult thing for us is —sending telegrams. Terribly difficult. Kindly listen.

(Taps on the table with his fork, imitating a telegraph key.)

REVUNÓV: What does that mean?

ZED: It means: Your Excellency, I respect you for your virtues. You think it's easy? Here's some more. *(Taps)*

REVUNÓV: Do it louder. I can't hear.

ZED: This means: Madam, how happy I would be if I were holding you in my arms!

REVUNÓV: Or else, if you're sailing in a high wind and need... and need to raise the topgallant and royal. Here the necessary command is: crosstree to the shrouds of the topgallant and royal and at the same time, as the sails loosen on the yardarm, below you make fast the sheets, halyards, and braces of the topgallant and royal.

ZED: *(Rises)* Kind ladies and gentle...

REVUNÓV: *(Interrupts)* There's all sorts of commands. Haul the topgallant and royal sheets over the halyards. But what does it mean and where is the sense? Very simple. It means haul the topgallant and royal sheets and hoist the halyards all at once. And also level the royal sheets and royal halyards on the upswing, and at the same time, as needed, slacken the braces with their sails, and then, when the sheets are hauled and the halyards all hoisted home, the topgallant and royal are stretched and the yardarm braced according to the direction of the wind.

NIÚNIN: *(To REVUNÓV)* Fyódor, the hostess asks you to talk about something else. The guests don't understand this and find it a little boring.

REVUNÓV: Who finds it boring? *(To APLÓMBOV)* Young man! Suppose a ship lies on a starboard tack under full sail and you've got to bring her before the wind. What's the command? Here's what: whistle up all hands on deck, veer about.

NIÚNIN: Eat now.

REVUNÓV: As soon as they all come running, I command at once: to your places, veer about. You give the command, and you see how the sailors run like lightning to their places and sort out topsails and braces. You can't help shouting: good lads...

(short pause)

ZED: And on this happy day, so to speak, when we have all gathered together to honor our beloved...

REVUNÓV: *(Interrupts)* And all this must be remembered. For example: foresail sheet, haul the main sheet.

ZED: Why do you keep interrupting? This way we won't be able to give a single speech.

NASTÁSYA: We're ignorant people, Your Excellency, we don't understand any of this.

REVUNÓV: Meat balls... Why do you call me Your Excellency? I'm not a general. Second-class captain is even lower than a colonel.

(pause)

NIÚNIN: Fyódor, but be so kind, allow us to call you Your Excellency. This family here, you know, is patriarchal, they respect superiors, they love high ranks.

REVUNÓV: Well, in that case, of course. We were remembering old times. You're sailing on the sea, knowing no grief, and... Do you remember the ecstasy, when you perform an about-ship? What sailor's heart doesn't light up remembering that manoeuvre? As soon as the command rings out: all hands on deck, about-ship—it's as if an electric spark runs through them all. Everybody's aroused, beginning with the commander, down to the last sailor.

ZMEYÚKINA: Make him stop...

General murmuring. NIÚNIN tries to serve REVUNÓV more.

REVUNÓV: I have food. Everybody's ready and their eyes are all fixed on the senior officer. To the foresail and mainsail braces to starboard, to the mizzen sail braces to port, to the counterbrace to port, commands the senior officer. Everything is done in an instant. Let go the foresail sheet, the jib sheet, hard to starboard. The ship rolls to windward, and the sails finally begin to fill out. The senior officer: the braces, mind the braces—and he himself fixes his eye on the main topsail, and when even that sail finally begins to fill out, meaning the moment for the about-ship has come, he gives the loud command: loose the main-top bowline, clear the braces. Here everything goes flying, flapping—Babylonian pandemonium. It's all carried out flawlessly. The about-ship has succeeded...

NASTÁSYA: If you're not a general, why did you take the money? And we didn't pay you that money to be outrageous.

REVUNÓV: What money?

NASTÁSYA: You know what money. You got twenty-five rubles from Niunin. *(To NIÚNIN)* And shame on you. I never asked you to hire the likes of him.

NIÚNIN: What's your point?

REVUNÓV: Hired... paid... What is all this?

APLÓMBOV: But, excuse me... Didn't you get twenty-five rubles from Niúnin?

REVUNÓV: What twenty-five rubles?

APLÓMBOV: So you didn't get the money?

REVUNÓV: I never got any money. How disgusting. How low. To insult an old man, a sailor, a decorated officer like this. Where's the door? Which way should I go? Someone show me out. Show me out. *(As he goes, being shown the way)* Disgusting.

(He goes out. Pause.)

ZMEYÚKINA: I'm suffocating. Give me atmosphere. I suffocate with you all around me.

ZED: You wonderful woman.

(ZMEYÚKINA begins to sing)

NASTÁSYA: Niúnin, dear, where are the twenty-five rubles?

NIÚNIN: *(to NASTÁSYA)* Why talk about such trifles? It's no big deal.

APLÓMBOV: Who needs meatballs?

ZHIGÁLOV: I'll have meatballs...

NIÚNIN: To the happy couple... so to speak...

(They eat)

LIGHTS FADE.

CHARACTER

IVÁN IVÁNOVICH NYÚKHIN

the husband of his wife, who runs a music school and a girls' boarding school.

NOTE

Underlined lines are from the speech he is preparing.

ON THE HARMFULNESS OF TOBACCO

A small room where IVÁN prepares his speech.

IVÁN: Dear ladies and, shall we say, gentlemen... It has been suggested to my wife that for charitable purposes I give a sort of popular lecture here. Of course, I'm not a professor and I'm a stranger to academic degrees, but even so it's thirty years now, without a break, one might even say to the detriment of my own health and so on, that I've been working on questions of a strictly scientific nature, reflecting, and sometimes, if you can imagine it, even writing scholarly articles, that is, not really scholarly, but, if you'll forgive the expression, in the scholarly line. Incidentally, the other day I wrote a mammoth article entitled "On the Harmfulness of Certain Insects." My daughters liked it very much, especially the part about bedbugs, but I read it over and tore it up. Because all the same, however much you write, it all comes down to insecticide. For the subject of my lecture today I've chosen, so to speak, the harm done to mankind by the use of tobacco. I'm a smoker myself, but my wife told me to talk about the harmfulness of tobacco today, so there's no arguing. I suggest, dear ladies and gentlemen, that you take my present lecture with due seriousness. I especially ask for the attention of the gentlemen doctors here present, who may draw much useful information from my lecture, since tobacco, apart from its harmful effect, is also used in medicine. For instance, if a fly is put in a snuff box, it will probably die of a nervous breakdown.

Tobacco is first of all a plant...

When I give a lecture, my right eye usually winks, it's from nervousness. I'm a very nervous man, generally speaking, and my eye started winking in 1889, on September 13th, the same day my wife gave birth, or whatever, to our fourth daughter, Varvara. All my daughters were born on the 13th.

(looks at his watch) In view of the shortness of time, we won't digress from the subject of the lecture.

I must point out to you that my wife runs this music school and a private boarding school, that is, not so much a boarding school, but something like that. Just between us, my wife likes to complain about not having enough, but she's got a bit stashed away, some forty or fifty thousand, while I haven't got a penny to my name, not half a penny—well, there's no discussing that. In the boarding school, I'm in charge of the housekeeping. I buy provisions, check on the maid service, write down the expenses, sew notebooks, exterminate bedbugs, walk my wife's dog, catch mice. Last night my duty was to supply the cook with flour and butter, because pancakes were planned. Well, in a word, today, when the pancakes were already made, my wife came to the kitchen to say that three of the girls were not going to eat pancakes on account of swollen glands. So it turned out that we had made a few extra pancakes. What was I supposed to do with them? My wife first told me to take them to the cellar, but then she thought, thought and said: "Eat the pancakes yourself, dummy." Whenever she's in a foul mood, she calls me dummy, or viper, or satan. But what sort of satan am I? She's always in a foul mood. And I didn't just eat, I gobbled them up without chewing, because I'm hungry. Yesterday, for instance, she didn't give me dinner. "There's no need to feed you, dummy," she says. *(looks at his watch)* We're babbling away and have gotten a bit sidetracked.

<u>Let's continue...</u>

Of course, you'd rather listen to a romance, or some sort of symphony or aria. *(Sings)* "We will not blink in the heat of battle..." I no longer remember where that comes from. I forgot to tell you that, in my wife's music school, besides housekeeping duties, I'm also responsible for teaching mathematics, physics, chemistry, geography, history, sight-reading, literature, and so on. My wife charges separately for dancing, singing, and drawing, though I'm the one who teaches dancing and singing. Our music school is located on Fivedog Lane, number 13. My life's probably such a failure because we live at number 13. My daughters were born on the 13th, there are 13 windows in our house. Well, what is, is. House number 13. Nothing has worked out for me, I've grown old, stupid. I look cheerful, but all I want is to shout at the top of my lungs or fly off somewhere to the ends of the earth. There's nobody to complain to, I even want to weep. You'll say: your daughters... What about my daughters? I talk to them and they just laugh. My wife has seven daughters. No, sorry, it's six. Seven. The oldest, Anna, is twenty-seven, the youngest seventeen.

<u>Dear ladies and gentlemen...</u>

I'm unhappy, I've turned into a fool, a nonentity, but in fact you see before you the happiest of fathers. In fact, this is how it should be, and I don't dare to speak otherwise. If you only knew.

I've lived thirty-three years with my wife, and I can say these have been the best years of my life, not the best, but generally speaking. *(looks around)* I thought I heard my wife coming.

Yes, so as I was saying...

My daughters have taken so long to get married, probably, because they're shy and because men never see them. My wife doesn't want to have dinner parties, she doesn't invite anybody to dinner, she's a very close-fisted, cross, cantankerous lady, and so nobody visits us, but I can let you in on a secret. My wife's daughters can be seen on big holidays at their aunt Natalya's, the same one who suffers from rheumatism and wears that yellow dress with black polkadots, as if it's been sprayed all over with cockroaches. Snacks are served. When my wife's not there, it's also possible to... *(Mimics drinking)*

I get drunk from a single glass, it makes me feel so good, at the same time so sad; for some reason I recall my youth and for some reason I want to run away, if you only knew how I want to run away, drop everything, run away without looking back. Where? It doesn't matter where. Just away from this paltry, banal, cheesy little life that has turned me into a pathetic old fool, a pathetic old idiot, run away from this stupid, petty, wicked, wicked, wicked skinflint, my wife, who has tormented me for thirty-three years, run away from the music, from the kitchen, from my wife's money, from all this pettiness and banality and to stop somewhere far, far away in a field, and stand there like a tree, a post, a garden scarecrow, under the vast sky, and gaze all night at the bright, quiet moon standing above you, and to forget, forget. How I'd like to remember nothing. How I'd like to tear off this shabby, wretched old suit jacket, in which I was married thirty years ago, in which I eternally give lectures for charitable purposes. *(takes off the jacket and throws it down)*

I'm old, poor, pathetic, like this jacket here, with its worn, mangy back. *(Shows his back)*

I need nothing. I'm higher and purer than that, I was once young, intelligent, studied at the university, dreamed, considered myself a human being. *(Glances aside)*

My wife is just there. She's checking on me.

(Quickly puts on his jacket)

Proceeding from the premise that tobacco contains a terrible poison, of which I have just been speaking, there should be no smoking under any circumstances, and I will allow myself, shall we say, to hope that my lecture "On the Harmfulness of Tobacco" will be of some benefit...

LIGHTS FADE.

CHARACTER

VASSÍLY VASSÍLYICH SVETLOVÍDOV

an actor, 68 years old

FEKLUSHA

a stage manager

SWAN SONG

The action takes place on the stage of a provincial theater, at night, after a performance. Night.

VASSILY, in bits of a costume.

VASSILY: Fell asleep in the dressing room. The show's been over for ages, everybody's gone, and I'm happily snoring away. I'm an old fart. What an old dog I am. Got so plastered I fell asleep sitting up. Clever idiot. Congratulations, dearie. *(Shouts)* Feklusha, Feklusha!... Today Feklusha got a fiver from me for her hard work—so now there's no finding her even with bloodhounds. Must've left and locked up the theater. I'm drunk. My God, the wine and beer I downed for tonight's show. My whole body's full of fumes, and it's like an army camped out on my tongue. Stupid, the old fool got drunk and doesn't even know why the hell. The lower back aches, the noodle's splitting, I've got chills all over, my soul's cold and dark, like in a cellar. Old age. No matter how I squirm, no matter how I pretend to be brave or play the fool, life's already been lived. Sixty-eight years, already bye-bye, best wishes. I can't bring it back. The bottle's been drunk, there's only a bit left at the bottom. Some sediment. Like it or not, it's time to rehearse the role of the corpse. Mistress Death is at hand. I've been on the stage for forty-five years, and this feels like the first time I've seen a theater so late at night. Damned interesting.

(Gets closer to the audience) Can't see anything. A black, bottomless pit, like a grave with death itself hiding in it. Cold. It's blowing from the hall like from a fireplace chimney. The most perfect place for calling up ghosts.

(Off a church bell chimes)

That's damned creepy. *(Shouts)* Feklusha! Where are you? My God, give up all these words, give up drinking, I'm old, time to die. At sixty-eight people go to church, prepare for death. But me, I come here.

(Seeing someone) What?

FEKLUSHA: *(entering)* It's me. Your stage manager.

VASSILY: Who? You? What are you doing here?

FEKLUSHA: I sometimes sleep in the dressing room. Sometimes I've got nowhere else to sleep.

VASSILY: Not a single soul thought of waking the drunk old man up and taking me home. I'm an old man, Feklusha. I'm sixty-eight. And I'm sick. I'm old, ailing, it's time to die. And I'm scared...

FEKLUSHA: It's time you went home, Vassily.

VASSILY: I've got no home—none, none, none.

FEKLUSHA: Have you forgotten where you live?

VASSILY: I don't want to go there, I'm alone there. I've got nobody, no family, no wife, no children. I'm as alone as the wind in a field. I'll die, and there'll be nobody to pray for me. There's nobody to keep me warm, to be nice to me, to put me to bed. Whose am I? Who needs me? Who loves me?

FEKLUSHA: The public loves you, Vassily.

VASSILY: The public left, they went to sleep and forgot about their buffoon. But I'm a human being, I'm alive, there's blood flowing in my veins, not water. Where has it all gone, that time, where is it? This pit ate forty-five years of my life, and what a life. I look into it now and see everything to the last little detail, like in your face. Youthful raptures, faith, passion, young love.

FEKLUSHA: It's time you were in bed, Vassily.

VASSILY: When I was a young actor, just beginning to feel passion, I remember—a woman fell in love with me for my acting. Graceful, slender as a poplar, young, innocent, pure and fiery as a summer dawn. The darkest night could not withstand the gaze of her blue eyes, and her wonderful smile. Waves from the sea break against stones, but cliffs, icebergs, snowdrifts broke against the waves of her locks. I remember sitting before her as I'm sitting before you now. I won't forget that look even in the grave. Tenderness, velvet, depth, youthful radiance. I fall on my knees before her, begging for happiness. And she... she says: abandon the stage. A-ban-don the stage. Understand? She was able to love an actor, but to be his wife? That day I played... It was a vile, buffoonish role. I acted and felt my eyes opening. I understood then that there's no such thing as sacred art, that it's all raving and delusion, that I was a slave, a toy of other people's idleness, a buffoon. Then I understood the audience. Since then I've never trusted applause... Feklusha, they applaud me, pay a ruble for my photograph, but for them I'm a stranger, for them I'm trash, almost like a kept woman. They seek my acquaintance out of vanity.

FEKLUSHA: Let me take you home.

VASSILY: My eyes were opened. And it cost me dearly. After that episode, after that girl. I started wandering around aimlessly, wasting my life, not looking ahead. I played buffoons, scoffers, I clowned, I corrupted people's minds, yet I was an artist, I had talent. I buried my talent, I trivialized and crippled my tongue. It devoured me, it swallowed me up—this black pit. Only now do I see my old age. My song has been sung. It's been sung.

FEKLUSHA: Vassily..?

VASSILY: Such talent, such power. You can't imagine such diction, how much feeling and grace, how many strings there are in this chest. That made me choke. Let me catch my breath. Here, this is from Lear. Dark sky, rain, thunder—rrr!... lightning—zhzhzh! ... across the whole sky, and me:

Blow, winds, and crack your cheeks! rage! blow!
You cataracts and hurricanoes, spout
Till you have drench'd the steeples, drown'd the cocks!
You sulphurous and thought-executing fires,
Vaunt-courriers of oak-cleaving thunderbolts,
Singe my white head! And thou, all-shaking thunder,
Strike flat the thick rotundity o' th' world!
Crack nature's moulds, all germens spill at once T
hat make ingrateful man!

Quick, the Fool, give me the Fool! Now!

FEKLUSHA: *(Playing the Fool)* O nuncle, court holy-water in a dry house is better than this rain-water out o' door. Good nuncle, in; ask your daughters' blessing. Here's a night pities neither wise men nor fools!

VASSILY:

Rumble thy bellyful! Spit fire! spout rain!
Nor rain, wind, thunder, fire, are my daughters.
I tax not you, you elements, with unkindness;
I never gave you kingdom, call'd you children.

Something else, something else like that. Let's knock off something from *Hamlet*. I'll begin... What with...? *(Plays Hamlet)* "O, the recorders! Let me see one. *(To FEKLUSHA)* Why do you go about to recover the wind of me, as if you would drive me into a toil?"

FEKLUSHA: "O! my lord, if my duty be too bold, my love is too unmannerly."

VASSILY: "I do not well understand that. Will you play upon this pipe?"

FEKLUSHA: "My lord, I cannot."

VASSILY: "I pray you."

FEKLUSHA: "Believe me, I cannot."

VASSILY: "I do beseech you."

FEKLUSHA: "I know no touch of it, my lord."

VASSILY: "It is as easy as lying. Govern these ventages with your fingers and thumb, give it breath with your mouth, and it will discourse most eloquent music."

FEKLUSHA: "I have not the skill."

VASSILY: "Why, look you now, how unworthy a thing you make of me. You would play upon me... yet you cannot make this little organ speak... Do you think I am easier to be played on than a pipe? Call me what instrument you will, though you can fret me, yet you cannot play upon me!" *(Laughs and applauds)* Where the hell is old age! There's no old age, that's all nonsense. Power spurts from every vein—it's youth, freshness, life. Where there's talent, Feklusha, there's no old age. Why are you crying? There's no old age, it's all humbug. Where there's art, talent, there's no solitude, no sickness, death itself is almost not there.

(Pause)

No, Feklusha, you are right. Our song is sung. A squeezed lemon, a sucked candy, a rusty nail, and you—a theater rat, a stage manager. Let's go...

(Pause)

In serious plays, I'm only good for crowd scenes now. And I'm too old for most of them.

(As they go:) Do you remember this from Othello ?

> **Farewell the tranquil mind! farewell content!**
> **Farewell the plumed troops and the big wars**
> **That make ambition virtue! O, farewell!**

They are gone.

An empty stage.

LIGHTS FADE.

ALSO AVAILABLE FROM SALAMANDER STREET CLASSICS

All Salamander Street plays can be bought in bulk at a discount for performance or study. Contact info@salamanderstreet.com to enquire about performance licenses.

CHATSKY & MISER, MISER!
translated by Anthony Burgess
ISBN: 9781914228889

Anthony Burgess expertly tackles the major monuments of French and Russian theatre: *The Miser* by Molière and *Chatsky* by Alexander Griboyedov. Burgess's verse and prose plays ***Chatsky: The Importance of Being Stupid*** and ***Miser, Miser!*** are published for the first time in this volume.

MEDEA by EURIPIDES
adapted by Kathy McKean
ISBN: 9781919483207

Kathy McKean's ***Medea*** reclaims Euripides' heroine in urgent, contemporary language. In Corinth, an outsider scorned and exiled, Medea faces Jason's betrayal and a society hungry to name her monster. With the audience as chorus, love curdles into vengeance, sacrifice and fierce self-definition.

HEDDA GABLER by HENRIK IBSEN
adapted by Kathy McKean
ISBN: 9781919483221

Kathy McKean's new version of Ibsen's ***Hedda Gabler*** crackles with sharp contemporary speech and bruising humour. Returning from honeymoon to a mortgaged house and a stifling marriage, Hedda seethes for agency. Old rivals, failed courage and loaded pistols spiral towards catastrophe, exposing desire, control and fear in a world watching.

Salamander Street

www.ingramcontent.com/pod-product-compliance
Lightning Source LLC
Chambersburg PA
CBHW022039090426
42741CB00007B/1126
9781068233494